If you were a

Conjunction

PICTURE WINDOW BOOKS
Minneapolis, Minnesota

by Nancy Loewen
illustrated by Sara Gray

conjunction (conj) a word that joins together other words or groups of words

Editor: Christianne Jones
Designer: Tracy Kaehler
Page Production: Lori Bye
Creative Director: Keith Griffin
Editorial Director: Carol Jones
The illustrations in this book were
created with acrylics.

Picture Window Books
5115 Excelsior Boulevard
Suite 232
Minneapolis, MN 55416
877-845-8392
www.picturewindowbooks.com

Printed in the United States
of America.

Library of Congress
Cataloging-in-Publication Data
Loewen, Nancy, 1964–
If you were a conjunction/by Nancy Loewen;
illustrated by Sara Gray.
p. cm. — (Word fun)
Includes bibliographical references.
ISBN-13: 978-1-4048-2385-3 (hardcover)
ISBN-10: 1-4048-2385-9 (hardcover)
ISBN-13: 978-1-4048-2389-1 (paperback)
ISBN-10: 1-4048-2389-1 (paperback)
1. English language—Conjunctions—Juvenile
literature. I. Gray, Sara, ill. II. Title. III. Series.
PE1345.L64 2007
428.2—dc22   2006003393

Looking for conjunctions?

Watch for the big, colorful words in the example sentences.

Special thanks to our advisers for their expertise:

Rosemary G. Palmer, Ph.D.
Department of Literacy College of Education
Boise State University

Susan Kesselring, M.A. Literacy Educator
Rosemount—Apple Valley—Eagan
(Minnesota) School District

If you were a conjunction ...

3

... you might be

lemon

sour

AND

sweet

watermelon

4

If you were a conjunction, you would be a connector. You would be the rope that ties ideas together.

I'll take the barbecued burger on a sesame seed bun

with a tomato **AND** lettuce,

2

BUT I don't want onions on the burger **UNLESS** they're fried.

7

If you were a conjunction, you could join single words or groups of words. You would be called a coordinating conjunction. You would be a word with two or three letters.

The brownies were warm **AND** gooey,

YET the milk was cold

AND refreshing.

The waiter served two pails of ice cream,

BUT it wasn't enough for our party.

The cake was gone, **SO** the monkey ordered banana bread instead.

Common coordinating conjunctions include and, but, or, nor, for, so, yet.

9

If you were a coordinating conjunction, you could turn two sentences into one.

Zach drank a big carton of milk.
He burped loudly.

Zach drank a big carton of milk, **AND** he burped loudly.

If you were a conjunction, you might work with a partner. You would be called a correlative conjunction. You and your partner would always work together.

PICK ME

PICK ME

EITHER a strawberry **OR** a pineapple would be fine.

Common correlative conjunction pairs include both/and, either/or, neither/nor, not only/but also, so/as, whether/or.

12

He wanted **NOT ONLY** mustard and ketchup, **BUT ALSO** relish for his corn dog.

RELISH

MU

If you were a conjunction, you could join two clauses. You would be called a subordinating conjunction.

I couldn't buy another treat **BECAUSE** I spent all of my money.

Since it was cold out, she bought a cup of hot soup.

15

If you were a subordinating conjunction, you could tell when things happen.

BEFORE

the pie-eating contest, Sally loved pie.

BEFORE

16

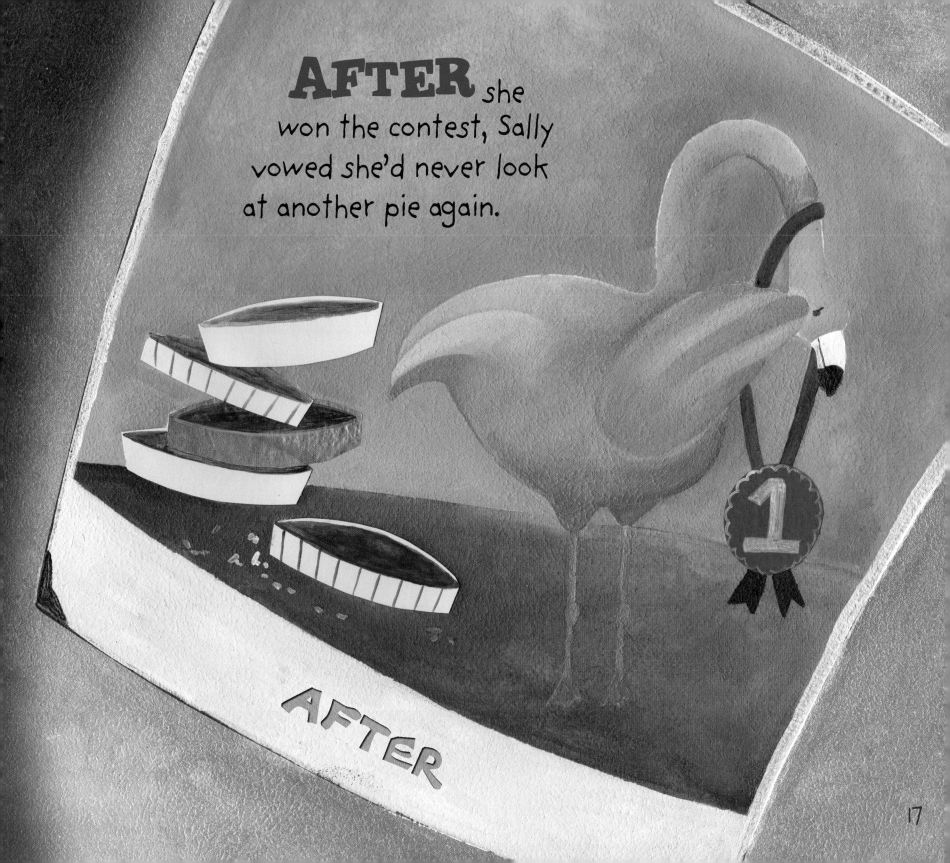

AFTER she won the contest, Sally vowed she'd never look at another pie again.

AFTER

If you were a subordinating conjunction, you could tell why things happen.

Edgar Elephant couldn't eat peanuts **BECAUSE** they gave him hives.

If you were a subordinating conjunction, you could tell how things happen.

Pedro gobbled
down the sandwich
AS IF he
hadn't eaten
in days.

21

You would be busy bringing things together ...

... if you were a conjunction!

Fun with Conjunctions

These unfinished sentences contain conjunctions.
Get together with your friends and see who
can come up with the craziest sentences!

Those pants are NEITHER _____ NOR _____.

Joe nearly missed the bus BECAUSE _____.

Karen hollered AS IF _____.

The casserole was made of _____ AND _____ AND even _____.

ALTHOUGH the chipmunk _____, we still enjoyed our picnic.

He threw popcorn into the air and caught it in his
    mouth WHILE _____.

MEANWHILE, back at the ranch, _____.

Are you done with these? Try making up your own.
Use the conjunctions in this book to get started.

Glossary

clause—a group of words that includes a subject and a predicate

coordinating conjunction—a conjunction that has just two or three letters and connects two separate sentences

correlative conjunction—a conjunction that always works with another word

predicate—a word or group of words that tells what the subject does or what is done to the subject

subject—a word or group of words that tells whom or what the sentence is about

subordinating conjunction—a conjunction that joins together two clauses to tell when, why, or how things happen

Index

To Learn More

At the Library
Heinrichs, Ann. Conjunctions. Chanhassen, Minn.: Child's World, 2004.
Heller, Ruth. Fantastic! Wow! And Unreal! A Book About Interjections and Conjunctions. New York: Grosset & Dunlap, 1998.

On the Web
FactHound offers a safe, fun way to find Internet sites related to this book. All of the sites on FactHound have been researched by our staff.

1. Visit www.facthound.com
2. Type in this special code for age-appropriate sites: 1404823859
3. Click on the FETCH IT button.

Your trusty FactHound will fetch the best sites for you!

Look for all of the books in the Word Fun series:

If You Were a Conjunction	1-4048-2385-9
If You Were a Noun	1-4048-1355-1
If You Were a Preposition	1-4048-2386-7
If You Were a Pronoun	1-4048-2637-8
If You Were a Verb	1-4048-1354-3
If You Were an Adjective	1-4048-1356-X
If You Were an Adverb	1-4048-1357-8
If You Were an Interjection	1-4048-2636-X